To †

Be Well
& Stay Green!
Aug '05

Green

Bamboo

Copyright 2005 by Joe Zarantonello

All Rights Reserved

Nirvana Press 2005

ISBN: 1-59872-021-X

Layout and design by Alida Coughlin
www.alidaDesign.com

Green

Bamboo

Selected Poems
by
Joe Zarantonello

2005

to Zia Maria — who introduced me to contemplation
without saying a word

Contents

What Matters	7
Be Well	8
Nothing	9
Death of the Western	10
Ritual	11
On the Dark Road	12
Wake Up Call	13
I Can Still Hear Him Laughing	14
Weapon of Mass Instruction	15
Shall We Dance	16
Green Bamboo	17
E-Mail From Stalin	18
Agnostic's Creed	19
Exhaustion	20
Fuck Viagra	21
Her Lucky Charms	22
Your Song of Mercy	23
Choosing a Dog	24
Dying to Take Your Hand	25
Pre-emptive Strike	26
Standing Ovation	27
By a Thread	28
Emergency Exit	29
A Round for Grief	30
Occupation	31
Legacy	32
Blizzard	33
Language of Life	34

Forty Hours Devotion	36
Walking the Bardo	37
Tonglen	38
Not Quite Empty	39
Why I Freewrite Every Morning	40
Eucharist	41
The Artist	42
Waiting for the Thunder	43
The Hunt	44
The Shroud	45
With the Grain	47
Still Life	48
Forever	49
To Go	50
Perfection of Character	52
Revelations	53
Each Gold Coin	54
One Reason	55
The Veil	56
At the Oars	58
Judo	59
The Big Dance	60
Titanic	61
Awakenings	62
Regarding Publication	63
The Big Lie	65
To the Brim	66
For All	68
Pure Joy	69
The Heart of Prayer	70
A Way of Ripening	72
Aged to Perfection	75

The Blind Man	76
The Centaur	77
Holy Folly	78
Noble Truths	79
A Stand	80
Sit There	81
Beyond the Grave	82
The Still Pond	83
New Wine	85
Taking the Bow	86
Far Horizon	87
State of the Union	88
A Gentle Proposal	89
For Rachel Corrie	90
Micro Gospel	91
The Gaze	92
Foot of the Cross	93
Dark Night	94
Everyone Belongs	95
Accordingly	96
Walking the Woods	97
The Green Man	98
Like Water	99
Merton's Bongos	100
Essential Teaching	101
The Only Road	102
The Little Dutch Boy	103
Lent	104
Nirvana	105
The River Wild	106
Fake It	107
Chemen Kwa	108

At Ninety	110
The Silent Treatment	111
Intimacy	112
The Real War on Terror	113
Vision	114
Imagine	115
By Your Side	117
The Land of the Pharoah	118
The End of the Line	119
Index	123

What Matters

It doesn't matter
if the world
chooses to accept
or reject your act of love.

It only matters
that you love the world
in the way
you were meant to love it.

Be Well

you can
drill
shallow
wells
here
there
and
every
where
or you
can
spend
your
life
drilling
one
well
until
you
strike
the
sweet
water
cool
and
clear
that
will
slake
your
thirst
forever

Nothing
(more or less)

when
i realize
simply
that
i am
enough

desire
& fear
drop out
from
the
equation
& i am
left
in
stillness
left
in peace
left
in joy
left
in love

left
to be
nothing
more
or less
than
what
i am

Death of the Western

How many movies have you seen
where the bad guy
rolls into town and hurts
some good people?
And then a good guy chases the bad guy,
catches up with him,
and blows him away?
And they all live happily ever after.

This is the Myth of Redemptive Violence.

The idea that somehow a bad thing
can be made good, that somehow
wrongs can be righted, by violence.
This myth died on Good Friday.
And it was killed by a man
who had seen through the myth,
and no matter what they did to him,
he had the courage to live and die
proclaiming forever the one reality of love.

Recently in Rwanda, a ten-year-old boy
told a missionary from Louisville,
"You know, Rwanda needs America,
but America also needs Rwanda."
When the American asked the boy
why he needed Rwanda,
the young boy replied
matter-of-factly—
"Because we've tried violence,
and we know that it doesn't work."

Ritual

the morning walk
with wu

every day
just before dawn

every day walking
the same old road

every day i stop
and bow

to the buddha sitting
under the beech tree

and wu pisses on it

On the Dark Road

I feel ashamed, even slightly obscene,
getting up before dawn
and driving 100 miles north
to a Benedictine monastery
to lead a Day of Natural Great Peace—
as smart bombs
rain down on Fallujah,
and men, women and children
are being gunned down
in the slums of Port Au Prince.

"How absurd," I think, as I put the car in gear.

And as I turn off our back road,
onto the county highway,
I see a fawn lying perfectly still
in a pool of blood
in the middle of the road;
and then my eyes
lock onto the doe eyes in the tall grass
just staring, unblinking
unthinking at my headlights.
I pass between them as slowly as I can.

Driving north, on the dark road of peace.

12

Wake Up Call

Woke up this morning feeling shitty, resentful and afraid
and then I began breathing the mantra in and out
and like lightning it struck me—hey fool, you are awake!
You are breathing! You have a bed to sleep in,
blankets to cover you! When you get up all you have to do
is flick a finger and the light will come on! Clean water
will flow from the tap. Still lying there in my bed,
tears of gratitude and joy begin to run down my face.
I continued breathing the mantra in and out for a minute,
for the Haitians, for the Iraqis, for all the homeless,
for all the poor of the world living in mansions on the hill
just dying for a practice as wonderful as this.

I Can Still Hear Him Laughing

for William Stafford

Columbian coffee, Tibetan yoga, even the mantra—
nothing seems to help on a morning like this.
I wake at 4, on mornings like this,
simply because you did. Visions and memories
of you sitting there in the dark Oregon night
bringing forth a poem every morning—
come hell or high water, on good days and bad.
And even on days when you had "the spiritual flu."

"I simply lower my standards on those days,"
You told Moyers. I can still hear him laughing.

Weapon of Mass Instruction

The secret weapon of Jesus and Gandhi,
of Martin Luther King and Nelson Mandella,
of Shirin Ebadi or Wangari Maathai,
and of all great human rights activists,
is simply the willingness to suffer loss after loss
again and again, until you win.

Shall We Dance?

It is so easy to fall into pattern or routine
after 30 years of marriage. As soon as
you begin to think that you know a person,
the musicians start packing up for the night
and they begin to mop the dance floor.

Who are you really?
What are your deepest desires?
When I can love you for your desires,
as if they were my own, only then
can the mysterious tango of souls even begin.

Green Bamboo

Just like green bamboo
In early morning fog

Our true selves flourish
In mystery

Darkness within darkness
Their essential soil

The silence between words
Lending them meaning
The space between planets
Enhancing their grace

True lovers must be empty
And have deep, deep roots

Just like green bamboo

E-mail from Stalin

> Date: November 3, 2004
> To: Karl Rove
>
>   comrade
>
>   you have learned well
>   the only rule—
>
>   those who cast the votes
>   decide nothing
>
>   those who count the votes
>   decide everything
>
>   kudos
>   joe

Agnostic's Creed

Don't know
Don't need to know
To become
Comfortable with Uncertainty

Don't know
Don't need to know
To relax
With the Great Surprise

Don't know
Don't need to know
The name of the Song
To begin tapping your toe

Don't know
Don't need to know
Any of the steps
When you're dancing with God

Exhaustion

Whenever I attempt
to do something
in a half-hearted way
I am greeted
by utter exhaustion.

It's as if each
and every cell
in my body
becomes a Mahatma
of passive resistance.

Refusing to work
in any cause
unworthy
of my whole
heart and soul.

Fuck Viagra!

Fuck Viagra!
Fuck abs and buns of steel!
Fuck the crazy arrested development
of human beings trapped in the Cult of Youth!

What does the seed know of the flower?
Or the sapling know of the giant redwood?

But what can you show
for a lifetime of facing death
every day on your little black cushion?

A soft belly, aching legs,
stretch marks, a sore ass, and perhaps
a heart broken into wholeness.
A luscious, generous ripeness, that is all in all.

Her Lucky Charms

Once again, the morning ritual—
waking up Elizabeth for school.
Wrapping my big robe around her,
telling her, "I love you, sweetheart."
Leading her out to the table, a bowl
of Lucky Charms, and a glass of cool,
clean water. She'll eat, and then go
back to bed "to snuggle" for awhile
until I wake up Pam an hour later.

Meanwhile, a world away from here,
the death squads "clean the streets"
of Port au Prince. In the middle
of the night, hooded men chase down
homeless boys just her age, wrestle
them to the ground, and then simply
shoot them in the back of the head.
They dump the bodies on the outskirts
of town, where they will be eaten
by feral pigs and packs of wild dogs.

I say it's a world away, but somehow
I know it is the same world. Somehow.

Your Song of Mercy

Whenever you get confused about
what you are doing here, or feeling
that you haven't amounted to much
in the way of the world—well, please
remember Kelty tapping his chest
and smiling.

Please remember that no matter what
your job or career is, your work remains
the same—to open that sacred heart
of yours to the radiant mercy of God.
And in return, to bear those beams of
love to each one you meet.

Choosing A Dog

Watching the Ohio Electoral College
cast their 20 votes last night on C-Span.
Watching Secretary of State Blackwell
braying like the donkey in Shrek about
how fair and honest and great the election
was. Watching each elector sign 6 copies
of federal affidavits in favor of Bush.

My yellow Lab, Wu, is a serious dog—
one who could keep the casual, drop-in
criminal in his car. Wu will sniff roadside
carrion for a long time, turning it over
and over, even tossing it in the air a few
times. But in the end, he won't eat it.

My kinda dog.

Dying to Take Your Hand

The body can live without food for weeks,
water for a few days, and air for a minute or two.
But the soul can't live for even a second without a meeting.

Don't get me wrong: men and women can endure
in quiet desperation for years, decades, even whole lifetimes.
But can you really call that living?

Take the time and a dime and scratch the formica of denial
and you'll reveal an ocean of despair, and beneath that, the soul
waiting patiently in silence, stillness and simplicity.

The one who's just dying to take your hand.

Pre-emptive Strike

Imagine a thousand squadron of Iranian
Air Force jets flying low over New York,
Atlanta and Cedar Rapids.
Over the Napa Valley and Crawford, Texas.
Persian Stealth bombers flying low
under the radar, dropping a million
copies of Hafiz, on America, simply for love.

Standing Ovation

Some days you just wake up weak
and afraid and muddled and think,
"What in the world is my life all about?"
On those days, it is hardest to sit down
at the blank page and bring forth.
Bring forth what? More doubt?
More despair? Who would want
to see that, in black and white, so early
in the morning?

These are the times—when the sound
of one hand clapping fills the night—
that no matter what you write,
the soul gives you a standing ovation.

By a Thread

Tragedies happen. Thugs in silk suits steal elections. Bad things happen to good people. Nothing you do can stop the suffering on this planet, in this country, or even in your own home. But you can sit, with all of it, in the silence. Back straight, eyes half-open, the thin golden thread of the breath leading you through the maze of dark emotion. One more time, saving the only life you can save; one more breath, breathing once, and for all.

Emergency Exit

There are thousands of ways to escape
from this virtual prison of the mind, back
into what people used to call "really living."

As many open windows, and as many
cell doors left ajar,
as there are stars in the Milky Way.

This towering inferno some call suffering,
and others call Hell, has millions
of emergency exits, all clearly marked: "Now."

A Round for Grief

Some days the grief just wins. Iraq,
the polar ice cap melting, Haiti,
the stolen election in Ohio, Merton
being dropped from the New American
Catholic Catechism—some days
you can take it all in stride. Face it all.
Grieve it all.

But yesterday, grief got the better
of me: the smell of diesel, the growling
of huge earth-movers cutting a road
across a virgin hillside. The farm that
borders our place. Old J.R. Barnes
used to sow that hillside in red clover
every winter. By the moon.

And now? Subdivision? Trailer park?
Kennels to hold suspected terrorists?
This morning, I just couldn't write about it.
I put the pen down, blew out the candles,
and went back to bed.

Score that round, unanimous, for grief.

Occupation

We live in an occupied country. A land not occupied
by Russian tanks, Islamic terrorists or Red Chinese—but by Wal-Mart,
Exxon-Mobil, Bechtel and Halliburton.

Fascism has nothing to do with swastikas or brown shirts.
It has everything to do with corporations ruling the country.
Most of our elected representatives are corporate shills.
And our twice-selected President is the ultimate, corporate hit-man.

Let's face it, we live in an occupied world. And justice for all will
take much more than an election. It will take decades of conscious
breathing—plus billions and billions of intricate, inner revolutions.

It will be a long haul. But there's no time, like the present, to begin.

Legacy

I look in the mirror and wonder, "Who is this
old guy staring back at me?"

What do you have to leave the children after
scores of years on this planet?

Black binder after binder of lines scribbled
in the dead of night?

Inky footprints of field trips through purgatory
to the holy land?

Yes, just that. And a faith tempered by experience,
that if you go as deep as you can into this life—

You can leave it all to the children with no regrets.

Blizzard

When farmers in the Great Plains
smelled a blizzard coming,
they would run a stout rope
from the farm house to the barn.

Grievous experience had taught them
how easy it was to wander off
in a white out and freeze to death.

The Eskimo have over 50 words
for snow. They know that blizzards
come flying every which way—
financially, emotionally, spiritually.

What is the rope strung between
your kitchen door and the barn?
Between the life you're living
and your soul's deepest desire?

Find out. Before it's too late.
Find out. Everything depends on it.

Language of Life

Every morning
tasting impermanence;

Biting through
the diamond silence,

Then swallowing
the moment of death.

                    Each

                    evening

                    the

                    white

                    empty

                    cup

                    brimming

                    with

                    new moon

                    light.

Then one utterly ordinary day,
sun rising on a shadowless cave.

The silent monk stumbles
down the mountainside
to the marketplace.

Dead trees, everywhere, bloom.

Forty Hours Devotion

Monday through Friday,
from eight to four,
the Body of Christ
is on exposition in my
classroom. Not enthroned
in a golden monstrance,

But slouching
slumped and formless
in an old, tatooed school desk.
Crucified each and every day
by acne, rage and uncertainty.
Holy, Holy, Holy.

Walking the Bardo

Walking the dark hallway between lives,
I stop in front of the closed white door.
My mother is behind that door,
sleeping, twitching, dying to teach us
all that she knows and cannot speak.

Walking the dark hallway between lives,
I stop again in front of her closed door
and bow a profound bow of gratitude—
just as the Trappists bow to the Eucharist,
just as the Zen monks bow to their zafus.

Walking the dark hallway between lives,
night after night I stop and bow, and
without warning, the white door opens.

Tonglen

for Pema Chodron

When gale-force
winds
blow in

And blue smoke
fills
the night

Climb the tallest
redwood
you can find

Strip yourself
naked

Open your arms
wide

And dance

Not Quite Empty

I wash last night's dirty dishes
every morning, often listening
to Coltrane or Ella, often listening
to you.

Sometimes a huge pile of dishes
to clean, but for me there is only
your beautiful begging bowl,
not quite empty.

The warm soapy water, the scouring
pad, the scalding rinse, the silence
of the drying rack.

How we go on.

Why I Freewrite Every Morning

Old Brother Juan once told me
that on the Appalachian Trail,
throughout the Smokies

The most magnificent
swallowtail butterflies—
tapestries in electric blue

Can often be found
fluttering
ever so gaily

Just above
the piles of horseshit
along the trail.

Eucharist

Sitting there with Mom, never close,
doing nothing. I look deep into her eyes
and I know nobody's home. For six
months, this scared the hell out of me.

But now, she is my Eucharist.
Simply because now, when I gaze
deeply into the void of her eyes, I realize
that the nobody I see there is me.

Simply because now, when I hold her hands
in mine, hands still as frozen doves,
I know truly, that this is my body.
Now I know, finally, that this is my blood.

So now, sitting here with Mom, staying close
and doing nothing; doing the work that truly
only nobody can do—I rest in the knowledge
that absolutely nothing is left undone.

The Artist

Clouds of gold
above
Basilica San Marco
only hint at the dawn
below
on the piazza.

The unholy riot
      of cigarette butts
and dirt
      empty Marlboro packs
bottle caps
and pigeon feathers

All bow to the street sweeper's
fluidity, his perseverance
and to his passionate indifference
as he begins his
slow, swirling tango
with the remains of the day.

Venice, 1996

Waiting for the Thunder

What is the sound of one hand clapping?

It is the sound of exile.
It is the sound of a tongue swallowed in fear.
It is the sound of what has been passing for my life.

The world is here, right here, hand outstretched
waiting, waiting, in the vast emptiness
of this information age.

The entire universe is waiting in beautiful stillness
hand outstretched, holding it's breath,
waiting in terrible silence

For the thunder of just your voice.

The Hunt

Orion hangs low
in the southern sky,
diamond sword dangling
like beckoning eyes

Just above the tops
of shrouded poplars,
as I begin another night walk,
another ritual.

What is the difference
between routine and ritual?
What is the difference between
"getting a life" and hunting one?

As if you could just walk right in
to Taco Bell and ask the girl
behind the counter for "One life,
extra large, minus the grief, please."

Near blind and crippled with arthritis,
Haiku still walks the dark road with me,
an old dog, but still moved
by visions of the hunt.

I began this poem
thirty thousand years ago
in the caves of Altimira.
It will never be finished.

The Shroud

for Dad

He was born in 1914,
the year of The Great War—
and he's been fighting it ever since.
Ever since, as a young Italian boy
in a German quarry town,
each and every day, fighting
his way to and from school.
Ever since, as a fiery youth
rebelling against his father
and refusing to be broken—
even after being locked up
with only bare bedsprings
and bread and water for weeks.
Ever since, battling his way
to the heavyweight title at ND
against men a hundred pounds heavier.
Ever since, he has fought every round, until now.

Now the bulging jockstrap
and boxing silks glistening with sweat
are retired—in favor
of plastic Depends and unmatched pajamas
smelling of urine.
Now, the angry hay makers
and raging body blows are gone.
The jabbing wit and the sparring profanity
are now all gone.
Now the steely blue fire in his eyes
is dimmed by grief's shadow,

and it doesn't even flicker
as the bell sounds the next round—
with the white bloody towel,
the shroud of the heavyweight,
now in the center of the ring
as his only answer.

With the Grain

I don't want to fade into the pastel sunset
> in Vero Beach with Barry Manilow
> playing softly in the background.

I don't want to look like Dick Clark, Ronald Reagan
> or even Liz Taylor.

I don't want to walk my two miles every day
> at the mall with all the usual suspects
> in The Golden Age Club.

I don't want to circle the wagons and get all
> my ducks and IRA's in a row to defend me
> against the ravages of uncertainty.

I don't want to spend my whole life erecting
> a Star Wars Defensive Shield to protect me
> from death.

No, I want to let my whole body age and weather
> like an unpainted barn—showing the blistering
> summer heat of loving, and the gray winters of grief
> in every board.

I want to load my pen, paper and poems
> into a rucksack and spend the day
> tramping the open roads.

I want to fan my tiny spark of existence into a blazing
> campfire under the blind night sky.

I want never to rage against the dying of the light,
> but instead, become a dancer in the darkness.

I want to live every day with my arms outstretched
> and nailed to the grain of experience, dying
> each morning into the innocence of dawn.

Still Life

for Mom

All your
rings
bequeathed
to other
fingers

And all your
teeth
rest white
and
silent
in a bowl

The song
now sung
by
many other
singers

But the
voice,
still yours,
sings
clearly
in my soul

Forever

On the morning we buried Mom

In the silence well before dawn,
sitting alone in a white plastic chair,
watching bubbles in the hotel pool.
Watching them stream from the aerator
and journey toward the center—
where one by one, they burst
and disappear into thoughts of Mom.

Success or failure?
Happiness or sadness?
Fulfillment or disappointment?
These thoughts all bubble to the surface
and fade—but what remains at the center
is the spirit of a person who faced it all.
Who lived it all with grace, a grace born
under the terrific pressure of life.

Terrific pressure is what turns
coal into diamonds, and it's what turns
human beings into saints—if we let it.
If we let it, God's will *will* be done—
and we'll all become who we really are
when all our bubbles have burst.

And even though diamonds really
aren't forever—saints, yes saints
are forever. And now, so is Mom.

To Go

You phoned
from
Maryland
from
your mother's
side.

I was
rushing
out
the door
out
to dinner.

We talked
awkwardly
without
really
speaking

All pauses,
all ellipsis.

Motors
revving
vehicles

heading
in
different
directions

Sometimes
you eat
dinner,
more often
dinner
eats you

Leaving
only a
starving
heart
and
one
thin
poem

to go.

Perfection of Character

Gazing out the window at the knobs,
covered with freshly fallen snow;
musing on a question posed by Sung-yuan,
late-twelfth-century Lin-chi master—
when I felt a chill in the house
and realized that I had let the fire die down.

So opening the wood stove, I began to poke
at the dead, gray ashes—much as Sung-yuan
prodded his dull students with this koan:
 "Why is it that someone of great satori
does not cut off the vermilion thread?"

The glowing coals exposed, I pile on the tinder
and kindling, and begin to blow, remembering
how in old China vermilion was a color
associated with women's undergarments—
and thus, with sexual energy.

The kindling breaks into flame with a loud crack,
and I load up the stove. The flames rush up the flue
with a deep, primal roar of a beast so necessary,
yet so dangerous, that you had better never forget
to shut the stove door.

Revelations

Early morning vigil at the Abbey. Black ink
rolling in waves onto white beaches of looseleaf
as the soul whispers words long unheard.

Four o'clock mass in the chapel with Kelty—
he flamencoes in wearing silver-toed cowboy boots
and dances through the ancient rite, timelessly—
like Ginger Rogers to Christ's Fred.

Later, constipated, coffee and book in tow,
I pay a visit to the throne room adjacent to
the guest house lobby. As I sit, I glance, amazed
at some ball-point penned graffiti just above
the handicap rail: "GOD LIVES!" it said.

No shit, I chuckled. No shit.

Each Gold Coin

for Crystal

Barely eighteen
and already a buddha—
sitting crosslegged,
breathing and smiling,
knowing and singing,
singing at last
from the mountaintop.

Clouds at your feet,
a mountain of gold coins
brilliant beneath you—
each gold coin the same,
each gold coin stamped
with grief on one side
and joy on the other.

Barely eighteen and
already an angel—
breathing and smiling,
knowing and singing,
barefoot and dancing,
dancing your way

Back home.

One Reason

I don't write for fun.
And I don't write for profit.

I don't write to analyze
And I don't write to anesthetize.

I don't write for vindication.
And I don't write for publication.

I don't write for popularity.
And I don't write for immortality.

I write for one reason.
And for one reason alone.

Resurrection.

The Veil

The veil
between
life
and
death
is much
thinner
than
we think.

One
moment
alive
and
the next
dead.

Thin.
Quick.

No fault,
just
pierced,
thin
veil
pierced.
(I have
time
everyone
thinks)

Will even
one
be
shaken
awake
by
her
death?

(I have
time
everyone
thinks)

At the Oars

ocean of glass
still
darkness at noon
not a breath of air
not a puff of wind
as men
in long boats
strain
at the oars
pulling, pulling
this huge four-master
inch by inch by inch
through
the
horse latitudes

Judo

Instead
of
trying
and
trying
to get
just
what
you
want
from
life

Instead
you
simply
try
over
and
over
to want
just
what
you
get

The Big Dance

There is nothing wrong with you.
I repeat, there is nothing wrong with you.

This chaos in your life
is absolutely normal.
It's just constant change.
It's just the way things are.
And the moment you begin
to recognize
that this chaos
is simply the voice of God;
and that you are meant
to be in it totally, but not of it;
only then, can you begin
to glimpse the Great Mystery.
Only then can you really begin
to join all of life in the Big Dance.

Things will never settle down.
Thank God, things will never settle down.

Titanic

You spend your life building your own
version of the Titanic, your own version
of an unsinkable luxury liner, impervious
to the heaving emotions below. And like
everyone else, you end up sooner or later,
stumbling onto the main deck at midnight,
waking in frozen disbelief, as all the things
you put so much faith in, slide past you
in one flickering, groaning moment—
swept away forever into the cold, dark night.
Only now, at the end, can you begin to see
the reality behind the illusion. Only now,
at the end, can you truly begin to love.

Awakenings

It's not
that
life's
so
short.

It's just
that
we're
so
darn
dead.

Most
of the
time.

Regarding Publication

Two letters to my sister, Camille

1.
On the back flap of
the envelope, you wrote in
longhand: "If you had
E-mail, you'd get more letters!"
I smiled. Yes, but then I'd miss

Your wonderful script,
and the two American
Holly stamps (slightly
askew) and your Coffee Time
logo which I love so much.
And I wouldn't be
as apt to shove your letter
into my pocket
for an hour or two, just to
savor the enveloping

Mystery of it all—
which is so perfectly you.
So I guess what I'm
saying is: I like your few
letters just the way they are.

2.
And that's exactly
how I feel about my own
poetry right now.

I still write for only one
reason—for resurrection.

Publication flows
from that as naturally
as a stream flows from
a spring. For without the stream,
the spring would become stagnant.

So yes, publishing
is important to me. And
that's why I publish
a hundred sets of poems
each New Year as gifts for friends,
And for the pleasure
and epiphanies as well.
And that is enough.
Enough to keep the sacred
spring refilling from below.

Besides, you closed your
letter saying you loved me,
that you recognized
the gift of me. Not even
Random House could guarantee

Bigger royalties!
Anyway, what's the big rush?
As you yourself mused:
"Grampa knew—the more dusty
the jug, the better the wine."

The Big Lie

Our personalities develop around a lie—
that the universe is out to destroy us.

We accept this illusion very early on:
at birth, or shortly after,
or even for some of us, in the womb.

Our personalities become our strategies
for survival in a hostile universe.
Some of us are Fighters.
Some of us are Pleasers.
And some of us are Hiders.

But all of us, all of us suffer because
these strategies just don't work.

The reason they fail
is simply because the universe
is, was, and always will be, friendly.

Buddhas, saints and mystics all realize this—
and have learned to live accordingly.

The kind winds of grace
gently beckon us to learn
only how to raise and trim our sails.

To the Brim

for Wilfrid Spratt, OCSO

Today I gifted
myself with sleep. Even the
most sacred rhythm
needs to be broken from time
to time, or the man begins
to be made for the
sabbath, not the other way
around. Twenty years
ago, in my wanna-be-
a-white-robed-monk phase, I was
having a devil
of a time staying awake
for Vigils. I just
couldn't seem to keep my eyes
open. So, one dark morning
I finally asked
this spry old monk who I met
rattling around
the refectory, "Brother,
do you attend Vigils?"
"Yes," he said. So I
continued, "Brother, I was
wondering how you
do this? I can't stay awake
no matter how hard I try!"

"Well," he smiled, "Do you
drink coffee?" "Oh no," I said,
"I don't do caffeine."
"Well, there's your problem. Nobody
does this stuff without coffee—
and lots of it! You
can be too pure, you know. Put
goldfish in distilled
water, and they'll die," he grinned—
filling his cup to the brim.

For All

I pledge remembrance
Of the Spirit
That is
The Unified Field of Consciousness;
And to the Kosmos
In which it Manifests—
One Taste
Of the Divine,
Indivisible
With Liberation
And Compassion for All.

Pure Joy

this
moment

minus
your

opinion
of it

The Heart of Prayer

*A Rendering of "The Lord's Prayer"
from the Aramaic*

O Beloved One—
Your oceanic womb births
Infinite blessing
In waves of shimmering light.

Each day we create
A space for grace and the dance
In our heart of hearts
Swept clean by your sacred word.

Dancing with Spirit
Like a feather on the wind,
Letting come what comes—
There's nothing we can't handle.

Our passionate hearts
Harmonize heaven and earth
By bearing the beams
Of Love to each one we meet.

Thank you for the food
To feed our body and mind,
And for the wisdom
To trust in your providence.

Untangle the knots
Of all misunderstanding,
And release our minds
Into the heart of mercy.

Forgetfulness will
Distract us from who we are,
So let us always
Practice remembrance of You.

O Beloved One—
Your glory shines within us,
Since before always
Our voices singing one song!

A Way of Ripening

*A Rendering of "The Beatitudes"
from the Aramaic*

Ripening are the Humble—
Who know
In their wisdom
That Sacred Breath
Is their only possession,
And that in this poverty
They are fully empowered.

Ripening are the Wounded—
Who breathe in
All the pain and loss,
And who breathe out simply
Some sense of relief
For themselves
And for all fellow sufferers.

Ripening are the Fluid—
Who greet
Whatever arises
As the river greets the rock:
With easy does it,
With around and through,
With the gentle way of water.

Ripening are the Zealous—
Who long for more
Than business as usual,
Who are truly hungry
For a clearer purpose in life,
And who will be satisfied only
By the sharing of heaven on earth.

Ripening are the Gracious—
Who birth
From their hearts
The glowing warmth
Of mercy and compassion,
Rekindling again and again
That most ancient cosmic fire.

Ripening are the Open—
Who were blind
But now can see everyone,
In the cloister
Or on the street corner,
Shining just like the sun
Of the one and only Original Face.

Ripening are the Empty—
Who can be peace
In the very midst of war,
Who can truly be
In the world but not of it,
And who can even become
Younger with each passing day.

And Wholly Ripe are the Lovers—
Who have dared
To dance beyond all social,
Racial and national boundaries
In joyful service and glorious
Wedding to the Beloved One.
They shall disappear without a trace.

Aged to Perfection

IT FINALLY DAWNED ON ME WHAT JESUS MEANT WHEN HE SAID: "BE PERFECT LIKE YOUR FATHER IN HEAVEN." I WAS WALKING DOWN THE ROAD, JUST BREATHING AND SMILING AT ALL THE NEW SNOW THAT HAD FALLEN DURING THE NIGHT.

LISTENING TO THE CRUNCH OF MY LUG SOLES ON THE DRY SNOW, WHEN IT DAWNED ON ME: THE WAY TO GROW OLDER IS TO IMITATE THE WAY THE UNIVERSE DOES IT!

MOST HUMAN BEINGS DON'T. MOST HUMAN BEINGS GET STUCK IN THEIR WAYS AT SOME POINT — AND BECOME MORE AND MORE RIGID IN HABIT AND BELIEF AS THEY GROW OLDER.

"GROW OLDER" IS REALLY AN OXYMORON. FOR IF YOU'RE ACTUALLY GROWING, YOU'RE LIKE THE VERY TIP OF THE BRANCH IN SPRING — NEW, SUPPLE, JUICY AND THE YOUNGEST PART OF THE TREE.

SO WHEN FACED WITH AGING, THE MODEL IS CLOSE AT HAND: THE UNIVERSE — EVER-CHANGING, EVER-OPENING AND EVER-GROWING — AS IT BECOMES YOUNGER AND YOUNGER AND YOUNGER TOWARD DEATH.

The Blind Man

The Gospel from the
Fourth Sunday in Lent was all
about the blind man.
Jesus mixed spittle with dirt
and rubbed it on the man's eyes.

And surprise—he saw!
After mass, and after lunch
you exploded in
rage and left the table, and
I felt just like that blind man.

'What the hell happened?'
the blind man yelled to his wife.
(Old tapes were running,
as she walked away from him,
invisible once again.)

My runaway bride—
the woman I had yet to
really see because
I'd been so busy looking
for my idea of a wife.

I can see that now.
And I have begun to glimpse
the magnificent
tapestry of a woman
that I was meant to marry.

The Centaur

Do you ride the horse?
Or does your wild horse ride you?
A basic question
everyone must ask, or else
you might just waste your whole life.

Our higher self is
human, our lower self is
an untamed, wild horse.
The greatest horse whisperer
who ever lived, died today.

He died to show us
how we must give everything
to learn how to tame
our wild cravings and desires,
how to school ourselves in love.

It's a Good Friday
only if we wake up and
accept the challenge
to become fully human,
to ride and not be ridden.

Holy Folly

So you don't know
What to do?

Well, big deal—
You don't *need* to know!

Just Listen to the Music—
Just Dance with the Mystery—
Just Do the Work—

And Trust
That God Will Provide.

Noble Truths

I
Life is challenging, suffering is optional.

II
Misunderstanding how to respond
To these challenges
Causes suffering.

III
An Enlightened Response is naturally
Present, Open & Fluid.

IV
The Awakened Ones practice Just This
By Dancing with each Moment.

A Stand

I will take my stand
With Jesus and the Buddha.
I will take my stand
With Gandhi and Einstein.
I will take my stand
With Merton and the Dalai Lama.
Standing with them
I firmly believe that peace
Can never be achieved by war.
Standing with them I say
There is no way to peace—
Peace is the way, now and forever.

Sit There

"I don't like war," you said,
"but I feel that we have to do something!"

But why? Isn't that just
our deepest American addiction?
Life happens, and we feel
compelled to react
by doing something—right now!

What if we followed the crazy wisdom of Zen:
"Don't just do something—
Sit there!"
What if we just sat on the ashes
at Ground Zero,
and wept and wept
until we could weep no more?

Perhaps that mighty river of grief
would cleanse our eyes,
or give us brand-new eyes
and the vision that America,
and the world, so desperately needs.

So please, don't just
Do Something—Sit There....
Until the ashes have grown cold,
and your tender heart of hearts catches fire.

Beyond the Grave

My old Zen master once said
that Nirvana was

"Seeing one thing through to the end."
Standing here at your grave,

reflecting on all our mad, crazy times
together

on all the darkness and light,
on all the cursing and blessing—

I grab a handful of dirt
and place it gratefully

on your coffin, knowing at last
that we

saw each other through.
Both of us now, beyond the grave.

23 March 2001

The Still Pond

The long
winding road
that wanders
through
the deepest
dark forest,
filled with
all the terrors
that only you
can imagine,
will finally
lead you
to a still,
shining pond.
When you
lean
over the edge,
all you can see
at first
is the soft glow
of a peace unknown.
As its soft light
draws you deeper
towards its source,
a long lost joy
bubbles up
to greet you.
And placing
a brilliant ring

on your finger,
it leads you
home—
to the
fathomless
radiance of love.

New Wine

They hung him on a tree because he was a poet.
Sure, he broke all the purity laws.
Sure, he upset the tables
of the money changers,
but in the end, it was his words.
The metaphor was what they couldn't handle.

Consider the lilies of the field?
Curse the barren fig tree?
Become one of the wise or foolish virgins?
It was all too poetic, too parabolic.
It was all too real. They called it blasphemy.
And they killed him for it.

"So how do you intend to make a living,
now that you're leaving the classroom?"

Well, captains of industry make decisions
like they make cars and make microchips,
like they make a killing, and a living.
Poets, on the other hand, don't make anything—
they sow. So no, I don't intend to make a living.
I'll grow one—one a hundred times richer.

A brand new wineskin for this brand new wine.

Taking the Bow

I
open
my eyes
and to
my surprise
find myself
paddling my canoe.

Perfectly synchronized
paddling.

No longer needing
to be
in control.
Allowing Life,
at last, to be
the stern paddler.

At long last,
for me, the
joy of
taking
the
bow.

Far Horizon

The most radical
thing you can do in this day
and age is simply
to give up all hope of gain
and all hope of fruition.
To do what you do
because it's what you are called
to do, and because
it is what you can do best,
but with no hopes for success.
It's so radical,
almost un-American—
to totally transcend
the bottom-line of mind,
for the horizon of soul.

State of the Union
Or the beginning of "Shock & Awe"

The Land of Lincoln,
Jefferson and Washington
is where I was born.
But now I sit in silence,
in the middle of the night,
hungry, rivers of tears streaming
from my eyes, nose and mouth.
No longer sitting
like purple mountain's majesty,
now I cower in holes
dug in gardens
by women and children,
and feel honored
to be among them, as things fall apart.

A Gentle Proposal

Go gently into the streets to protest the war.
Go gently into discussions with your neighbor
about the price of oil and human life.
Go gently into your own kitchens and living rooms,
into your schools and workplaces.
Go gently into your houses of worship,
into your hospitals and prisons.
Go gently into your opinions of world leaders.
And go gently, ever so gently, into your own mind.
Otherwise, what have you really accomplished?
If you go with aggression, you may win the battle
but you won't stop the war—for aggression is war.
All wars are lost as soon as they're begun.
So go gently into the very thick and heat of battle.
Go gently, and even if your cause does not prevail,
there will be more peace, in the world, than before.

For Rachel Corrie

What if the American girl
who knelt in protest
in front of the house
of a Palestinian doctor
in the West Bank
(and was crushed
by an Israeli bulldozer)
what if she didn't lose her life
in that awful moment,
but win it?

What if all of us,
living on the edge of war,
came out of our comfortable foxholes,
spread our arms wide
and lived as if we really believed
in the power of the cross?

What if suffering
really is
the fastest horse to God?

Micro-Gospel

The Beatles were wrong
When they sang,
"All you need is Love."
There is no need.
No need.
"All there is, is Love—
And our resistance to it."

The Gaze

One way or another, our
entire personality is a
vast project
to get others to love us.

What happens
to that project when we
realize by faith, that God is
always bathing us
with His loving gaze?
That we always already
have what we seek?
What happens
when I realize
that God is the eye
with which I look for God?

"Build it and they will come?"
No. Empty it—and you will
become
the Living Gaze of Love.

Foot of the Cross

What do we do when
the one's we love suffer?
What do we do when
we find ourselves standing
at the foot of the cross?

I used to pray for an end
to the suffering. But now
I pray that my friend
will breakthrough to the truth.

For life has taught me
that truth
always lies waiting
on the far side of suffering.

And that the fastest way
to the truth,
is to say "Yes"
to the suffering at hand.

Heaven just might be
a perpetual state of
"Yes!" Breakthrough
after breakthrough
into the surprise of God.

Dark Night

The breakdown of the ego—
and the emergence of the god-seed through the rubble.

The lack of success is all part of the purification process.
The feeling of personal failure, the despair,
hopelessness, depression—all of it.

I need to go deeper within.
Really trust the process I've been given.
Use my own way—let my life lead.
I keep looking for the "lost key" out here on the front lawn,
because the light is so much better out here.
But the truth is, the key is right where it's always been—
in the house, in the cave of the heart,
in the darkness of night.

Everyone Belongs

When your longing changes
your life changes
with it.

I used to long to be
happy and safe
forever.

But somehow,
despite my ego's
best efforts,
my longing
was transformed—

Into a longing for
just this moment

Into a longing for
the next surprise

Into a longing for
the deepest truth.

Everyone belongs
to their longing
whether they
know it
or not.

Who or what
will you
belong
to?

Accordingly

When fear arises
and grips
your very soul,
can you remember
who you are
and who God is?

And then with
a single breath,
and a simple smile,
renew your vow
to live your life
accordingly?

For you cannot
think your way
into
a new way
of living.

You can only
live your way
into
a new way
of thinking.

This is one way
that perfect love
can drive out
all fear.

This is one way
that you can
pray
without ceasing.

Walking the Woods

Like a zombie searching for a sip of salt water,
I ramble through the old forest in winter.
The trees all look quite dead,
but always, beneath the surface
resurrection patiently awaits its turn.

The trees have always known
how to "winter over." The trees have
no word for hope. They just winter
the cold and ice, snow and darkness,
ripening in the knowledge of spring.

When, when has spring ever failed to come?
Hoping leads to depression; knowledge
leads to patience, wisdom and compassion.
I walk the woods to forget myself,
and to remember, all of this.

The Green Man

The Green Man built a tree house in the center of my heart.
No one asked him to. He just showed up one day.
He never asked me. He never called to inquire
about available space. The Green Man just appeared
one day, swinging and laughing
in a glowing tree of emeralds in the heart of my chest.
I forget all about him, and then when pain or suffering arises,
I can hear him laughing and swinging from the branches,
and somehow that changes everything.
More and more, I open my heart to the pain
and suffering of the moment, and just breathe it all in.
On the out breath, a green luminosity
vibrates out into the world from every cell in my body.
The green of a newly unfurled leaf on the first day of spring.

Like Water

Let your self
assume the shape
of the moment
you are being poured into.
Become like water.
A styrofoam cup,
Waterford crystal
or an old, plastic bedpan—
it's all the same to water.
Divorce your preferences
and marry your longing.
Let this be your true spouse.
Let this be your gravity.
Then the only control
you will ever need
in any situation
is the situation itself.
So follow your longing
and become just like water.

Merton's Bongos

On that September afternoon
when Gene Meatyard
snapped a photo of you
wailing away on the bongos—
your smile said it all.
No longer Merton,
no longer the pious, young
monk climbing seven
storied mountains to heaven.
No, all that was forgotten.

Forgotten, in that
one glorious and shining
holy calypso
moment. Forgotten, at last,
as shadows blurred into light.

In a week you would
leave Gethsemani for good.
A monk without a monastery,
dancing your way
to the far east and home.

But you knew by then that
we are all somebodies
just dying to be everybody.
And that we are all
monks without monasteries

Whether we know it or not.

Essential Teaching

Confucius and Chuang Tzu sat on the bank of a frozen river sipping tea. Confucius asked, "What is the essence of teaching?" A half-smile rose to Chuang Tzu's lips, he drank his last bit of tea, washed the cup out with snow, carefully placed it upside down on the tea mat, arose and walked on down the ice toward the sea. Not a crow cawed, not a mouse stirred, not a word was heard from his footprints in the new snow.

The Only Road

Personalities can't love—
they want something.
Either the fulfillment of hopes
or protection from their fears.
True love for another
can only be found
by traveling the road
to the deep interior—
by realizing that nothing's been lost
and nothing is needed;
that there is nothing to hope for
and that there is nothing to fear.
It's a long road, but the only road
that can lead you to the path of love.

Little Dutch Boy

The Little Dutch Boy
finger still in the dike
after all these years,
holding a tattered copy of Rumi
in his other hand,
realizes all at once —
that if he keeps his finger
in the dike forever,
or pulls it out right now,
either way, it doesn't matter.
God loves him, and there's not
a damn thing he can do about it.

Lent

Enlightenment in the river Jordan is all well and good
with the sky opening and doves and voices and all
but 40 days in the desert is another thing entirely.

To go into the desert with the wild beasts
and the angels. Not just one, but both.
Even just the wild beasts
would have been easier, simpler.

After enlightenment, the complexity.
Living your dream isn't easier than living
someone else's nightmare. It is more
fun, but it isn't easier, it isn't simpler.
Living someone else's dream,
which is a real nightmare,
is often the simplest thing you can do.

Lent is a call to dream your own dream again.
To let the golden hair of the angel
and the rough black fur of the beast
be woven into a tapestry of what your life means to be.

Nirvana

When asked
to define
Nirvana,
the Buddha
replied,
somewhat
enigmatically:
"Not suffering."
The cessation
of suffering
does not mean
the cessation
of all pain.
But rather,
it means
the cessation
of all struggle
against the pain.

The River Wild

As things fall apart, as the deeps
begin to quake, as fault lines
in the body and the body politic
begin to shift—somehow,
what begins to emerge
is a deeper brand of courage.

Courage that is no longer tied
to succeeding, no longer
needing to win or even survive.

A river wild with compassion
and raw openheartedness
that has jumped its banks,
that has burst through the dams,
that is at long last married
to the vast, bittersweet ocean.

Fake It 'Till You Make It

It's the end of this world and the beginning of the next
the moment you realize in the marrow of your soul
that no matter what happens—you will be taken care of.

It won't matter then, if you live in splendor or poverty.
If you live in the mansion on the hill, or under the overpass.
You will be taken care of, no matter what.

The day you truly feel that, in each and every cell,
is the first day of the great freedom.

Chemen Kwa*

for Marguerite Laurent

I just can't imagine getting
phone calls from Haiti—
from people you know
in Bel-Air
or Cite Soleil
pleading for help
(with gunfire
or screams
in the background)
on cell phones
that suddenly go dead.

It must be utterly
excruciating
bathing
the feet
of each
Kreyol Christ
with your tears,
and wiping
them dry
with your hair
day after day,
year after year.

May all your anger,
grief, tears

and despair
be
transformed
into even
more
courage
perseverance
and compassion.

*"The Way of the Cross" in Kreyol

At Ninety

for Matthew Kelty OCSO

four a.m. mass
of the zombies
after vigils
with kelty
mano a mano
nobody but jesus
and matthew
in mondrian
crescent moon
vestments
and house slippers
shuffling
through the mass
at ninety
like gene kelly
still singin'
in the rain
may the body
and blood
of christ
bring us all
to everlasting
life

The Silent Treatment

When I get angry,
before I even know what's happened,
I am giving someone I love
the silent treatment.

Even though in my heart of hearts
I have vowed to be
present, open and fluid
like the Buddha.

But when I don't get what I want,
or when I get a whole lot of what I don't want,
before you can say Shakyamuni—
I'm in bed, drowning in covers and resentment.

As if laying there
drinking poison in the darkness
would hurt them.
As if it ever, even once, helped me.

Intimacy

No longer worshipping the jade stem
or the dark, misty valley.
The ear of the heart becomes the virgin
and the word becomes seed.
The desperate need for confirmation fades
with the dawning of true communion.
There *is* something better than sex
or chocolate.

The Real War on Terror

The real war on terror begins in the heart.
Look deeply within your own heart
and see the frustration, the resentment.
See the anger and the hatred.
And then, look even deeper into your heart,
below all of that, and see the fear—
the utter terror that poisons the water
at the very bottom of the well of the heart.

Until you find, understand and uproot
the terror that hides so completely
in the cave of your own heart,
there will always be
another Bin Laden or Bush.
As the Dalai Lama has so often said,
the greatest enemy that he ever faced
was not Mao—it was his hatred of Mao.

Vision

for John Coltrane & Yvon Neptune

Struggle without vision
is slavery. It's a kind of
slow torture.
Vision without struggle
is mere fantasy,
a kind of
pie in the sky
in the great by and by.
But a vision and
the willingness to struggle
to make it a reality—
that is a love supreme,
and that
is the salvation of the world.

Imagine

Imagine a life
of happiness,
perfectly
fulfilled
and
satisfying,
wholly
integrated
and
meaningful.

What would
it
look like?

What would
you
be doing?

Who would be
sharing it
with you?

If you can't
even
imagine
this kind
of life,

how could
you ever,
ever
hope
to live it?

By Your Side

In Tibet they would never dream
of leaving their loved ones
to travel the bardo alone.
Whether it is at the moment of death,
or some other dark, tumultuous
period of serious transition—
a dharma friend will always be there.
So no matter how crazy it gets,
please always count on me
to be right there by your side,
either in flesh or in spirit,
gently whispering the teachings
into your ear, and reminding you
again and again and again
that you are always and already
the jewel in the heart of the lotus.

The Land of the Pharaoh

We all have to escape from Egypt.
We all have to walk across the Red Sea to freedom.
And then still, it'll be forty years of wandering in the desert.

Slavery is steady work. It may be abuse, but at least
it's predictable—three hots and a cot is something to lose.
Almost anything seems better than wandering in the desert.

But remember, there will be a cloud to follow by day,
a pillar of fire by night,
and bread falling like the dew every morning.
And eventually, there will be milk and honey. But only
if you believe enough to finally leave the land of the Pharaoh.

The End of the Line

All my years of training as a poet
have taught me this: to sense where
one line ends and the next begins. It's about
as easy as it is to sense where winter ends
and the spring begins. Things
tend to bleed into each other. Life
gets messy. Other voices and other views
tend to muddy the water.

But in the early morning, well before dawn,
in the deep silence of the night vigil,
if you listen with every cell of your body—
you'll know. You'll know.

About the Author

Joe Zarantonello is a teacher, poet and the creator of *The Integral Journal*. Joe's undergraduate degree is from the University of Notre Dame where he majored in The Great Books. His M.A. is from University College (Dublin) where he studied the Irish poets.

Joe spends most of his time at home, with his wife Pam, running Loose Leaf Hollow—a guesthouse for solitary or guided retreats in the rolling knobs outside of Bardstown, Kentucky.

This poem is framed and hangs on the wall beside the door at Loose Leaf Hollow—

My Passion

My vocation
And my avocation
My work
And my play
Is helping others
Create a way
To bring forth
Their hidden brilliance

Index

A

A Gentle Proposal	89
A Round for Grief	30
A Stand	80
A Way of Ripening	72
Accordingly	96
Aged to Perfection	75
Agnostic's Creed	19
Artist, The	42
At Ninety	110
At the Oars	58
Awakenings	62

B

Be Well	8
Beyond the Grave	82
Big Dance, The	60
Big Lie, The	65
Blind Man, The	76
Blizzard	33
By a Thread	28
By Your Side	117

C

Centaur, The	77
Chemen Kwa	108
Choosing a Dog	24

D

Dark Night	94
Death of the Western	10
Dying to Take Your Hand	25

E

Each Golden Coin	54
E-Mail From Stalin	18
Emergency Exit	29
End of the Line, The	119
Essential Teaching	101
Eucharist	41
Everyone Belongs	95
Exhaustion	20

F

Fake It	107
Far Horizon	87
Foot of the Cross	93
For All	68
For Rachel Corrie	90
Forever	49
Forty Hours Devotion	36
Fuck Viagra	21

G

Gaze, The	92

Gentle Proposal, A 89
Green Bamboo 17
Green Man, The 98

H

Heart of Prayer, The 70
Hunt, The 44
Her Lucky Charms 22
Holy Folly 78

I

I Can Still Hear Him Laughing 14
Imagine 115
Intimacy 112

J

Judo 59

L

Land of the Pharaoh, The 119
Little Dutch Boy, The 103
Language of Life 34
Legacy 32
Lent 104
Like Water 99

M

Merton's Bongos 100
Micro Gospel 91

N

New Wine 85
Nirvana 105
Noble Truths 79
Not Quite Empty 39
Nothing 9

O

Occupation 31
On the Dark Road 12
One Reason 55
Only Road, The 102

P

Perfection of Character 52
Pre-emptive Strike 26
Pure Joy 69

R

Real War on Terror, The 113
Regarding Publication 63
Revelations 53

Ritual	11
River Wild, The	106
Round for Grief, A	30

S

Shall We Dance	16
Shroud, The	45
Silent Treatment, The	111
Sit There	81
Stand, A	80
Standing Ovation	27
State of the Union	88
Still Life	48
Still Pond, The	83

T

Taking the Bow	86
The Artist	42
The Big Dance	60
The Big Lie	65
The Blind Man	76
The Centaur	77
The End of the Line	119
The Gaze	92
The Green Man	98
The Heart of Prayer	70
The Hunt	44
The Land of the Pharaoh	118
The Little Dutch Boy	103
The Only Road	102
The Real War on Terror	113
The River Wild	106
The Shroud	45

The Silent Treatment ... 111
The Still Pond ... 83
The Veil ... 56
Titanic ... 61
To Go ... 50
To the Brim ... 66
Tonglen ... 38

V

Veil, The ... 56
Vision ... 114

W

Waiting for the Thunder ... 43
Walking the Bardo ... 37
Walking the Woods ... 97
Wake Up Call ... 13
Way of Ripening, A ... 72
Weapon of Mass Instruction ... 15
What Matters ... 7
Why I Freewrite Every Morning ... 40
With the Grain ... 47

Y

Your Song of Mercy ... 23